101
STEPS TO MAKING
VIDEOS LIKE
A PRO

C.C. CHAPMAN

&

MARK YOSHIMOTO NEMCOFF

Wordsushi Books

a division of Glenneyre Press

Los Angeles, CA

ISBN: 1-934602-37-X
ISBN-13: 978-1-934602-37-9

Published by Wordsushi Books
a division of Glenneyre Press, LLC.
Los Angeles, CA
www.wordsushi.com

First Edition

Cover design by: MYN

WHY SHOULD I CARE WHAT THESE GUYS HAVE TO SAY?

C.C. CHAPMAN

Ever since I saw my grandfather's homemade 8mm reels on our projector I was in love with movies. While attending Bentley University, my roommate and I formed Random Foo Pictures. We'd go on to produce 74 shorts and 2 features. We were one of the premiere production companies in the early days of microcinema, and I even took home a Best Director and Short of the Year award for our work on 'Inquisition.'

I was one of the first wave of bloggers and podcasters. Hosting the most popular independent music podcast in the world lead to being paid to record and the show being on Sirius. I'd go on to help a friend launch an agency and then would launch my own. My clients have included American Eagle Outfitters, HBO, Verizon FiOS, Snapple, Warner Brothers, Subway and The Coca-Cola Company.

In 2010, I co-authored the International best-seller *Content Rules*, still considered by many to be the bible of content marketing. My photographs, words and thoughts have appeared in Rolling Stone, the Wall Street Journal and on CNN. As a Keynote Speaker I've addressed thousands from stages around the globe, including most recently in Istanbul and The Netherlands.

Amazing Things Will Happen could be a motto for my life, but it is also the title of the book that I wrote in 2012. I make a living advising companies and organizations how to be better storytellers. I explore the world for both pleasure and humanitarian efforts and always capture and share the stories I find. You can see, read and experience my latest at CC-Chapman.com

MARK YOSHIMOTO NEMCOFF

So much of my life has been tied to moving pictures. My father ran the newsroom at Channel 10 in Philly, where I spent a lot of my early childhood running around the TV studio and tripping all over the wires. Later, after he went on to win documentary awards and shoot films for companies far and wide, I spent my share of summer vacations carrying tripods and holding up bounce boards, for no pay either. Once during college, I was a production assistant for a Japanese news crew shooting around Florida, which was an adventure. I worked creating interactive touch screen pilot training videos in 1990. I didn't even have my own computer in 1990.

I've composed original music for network TV and major video games. I was a free-lance writer on Pam Anderson's massive hit syndicated show, "VIP", the same year I was picked for the Warner Bros. Drama Writer's Fellowship. I've penned feature film scripts on assignment. I've covered big music events for Blender. For a while I was the assistant to a big TV music composer, where we did several hit sitcoms and then ended up running all the business affairs for the company.

At some point, I started a podcast in my car that ended up as an evening drive-time radio show on Sirius five nights a week. Playboy Magazine even wrote about me. That show even spawned a video show which eventually landed me a gig hosting, writing and co-producing a nationally-syndicated TV series about smartphones and mobile technology and entertainment. I've hosted on-camera for big events and major Hollywood red carpet premieres.

I've written a bushel of books that have sold very well on Amazon through the publishing imprint I founded in 2005. I'm proud of that, and also very proud that one of my books has achieved a lot of major media exposure, even landing me as a featured commentator on E! Entertainment's series, "Secret Societies of Hollywood".

I've moonlighted as a branding consultant for big tech firms like GoDaddy and Verisign, and stealth advised a few companies through some big social and commercial campaigns.

Today, you can also hear me on TV and the radio, in video games and product videos all around the world, as I have become a busy VO artist, voicing spots for BMW, Ford, McDonalds, Coca Cola, Chevy, Mercedes, Dominos, Pizza Hut, JetBlue, Honda, Kia, HP, Volvo, GameFly, Stella Artois, Universal Music Group, Jeep and many other brands big and small.

You can find Mark online at Wordsushi.com

For every person, brand or business out there
who wants to make videos...
but doesn't know where to start.

TABLE OF CONTENTS

YOU WANT TO MAKE VIDEOS...

Far beyond merely being transformative and disruptive, video on the web has become a kinetic force of nature — hugely influential due to the tremendous level of engagement and response it generates—far more powerful than any other current form of media. Because most Internet video can be enjoyed and shared through practically every smartphone, tablet and laptop on planet Earth, it has the potential to cast a global spell at the speed of electrons. That is some serious mojo.

Like many of you, even from a very young age, we were the ones enamored with the idea of somehow being on television or in the movies. Funny thing is that each of us, in our own way, ended up spending a good portion of our teenage, college and adult days on both sides of the camera and behind the scenes. We understand the current digital media landscape and, between us, share decades of professional experience planning, shooting, editing videos, positioning our content online in front of audiences and socially marketing the heck out of it all. We get it.

What you say is still as important as how you say it and how you present it. That wonderful social sharing of your content creates and deepens bonds between you, or your brand, and your fans and, through them, reaches their social circles and beyond. Smart brands and media-savvy creatives realize they have *audiences,* not just customers, and creating videos has never been easier—or more challenging.

We live in an age when the dominance of the television, as the most-watched form of entertainment, has fallen into the rear view mirror of modern reality. In our ever-expanding universe of social engagement, you can no longer just rely on all the same old techniques to get noticed and still expect exponential results. If you're a small (or large) business, you either already know how essential video content has become to a social-media hungry world, or you're doomed to be a 'horse and buggy' brand in a Jetsons' universe.

The idea of being on camera is appealing for every reason you can think of, and some that you may not have imagined yet. For others, the draw comes from using a camera to tell a story or elicit emotional responses. Thanks to YouTube, anyone can write, create and be in the movies!

Not long ago, it was easy-peasy. The technology and tools to make videos became cheaper, faster, to the point where all you need to get started is an idea (or a stupid decision) and your phone and you could have the next great viral video. Now, with more and more media creators and brands making videos to get their messages seen by the digital-savvy content consumer, your success doesn't just depend on knowing what you're doing, but also deftly navigating the path from start to finish.

We are not here to teach you about viral videos. We are not here to talk about cat videos. In fact, we don't care what kind of videos you want to make. We just care that you make them look, sound and entertain as much as possible. We're not going to be those guys who attempt to hypnotize you with a bunch of mind-blowing media stats about the overwhelming popularity and penetration of Internet video among today's digitally-actuated consumers, because that's exactly the kind of thing salespeople throw at you to make you feel like you're missing out and, as such, scare you into feeling insecure so you'll buy their solution.

We're here to empower your self-confidence when it comes to making videos, not undermine it. We know the tools and resources you can utilize to make your own videos, or just make them better, are out there. We just want to help you find them and use them to their fullest advantages.

We can't tell you we know how to make you famous overnight, and we are not going to tell you that successfully producing videos for the Internet is easy because that would be a dirty fib. We'll be the first to tell you that creating videos offers its own unique set of challenges. Truth is, making Internet videos is actually not as difficult as it may seem at first blush. You don't have to feel like you're in over your head, or that having an effective video strategy is a luxury you can't afford when you know how to think like a pro.

And the rewards? What could be better for any aspiring video maker than to find her or his audience or, for a growing business, to have a constant reminder of their brand spooling back on the screen of a mobile smartphone user searching for whatever it is that they do?

After years of talking about doing a book like this, and finally growing sick and tired of all the bad advice out there, we've finally pooled our years of knowledge to pass it on to aspiring video makers like you. We even tapped a few of our expert video creator and marketing friends for the kind of valuable pro tips that are only gleaned from decades of experience in the trenches.

We have been in your shoes. It's because someone laid out a breadcrumb trail for us to follow down our own paths for success that we feel inspired to break down the process of making videos into a blueprint you can follow to plan, shoot, edit, upload and market your video like a pro.

≈ *PRO TIP* ≈
SCOTT MONTY

Whenever possible, frame your video as something that will provide value or otherwise benefit the viewer. Don't make it about you and what you're showcasing. Of course, that means the video itself needs to reflect that thinking.

Scott Monty, Global Head of Social Marketing for the Ford Motor Company

≈ *PART 1* ≈
PLAN TO MAKE VIDEOS LIKE A PRO

At minimum, you'll need a camera, someone to stand in front of it and someone/someway to operate it. And if you are the on-screen talent and the cameraman as well, congratulations, you've simplified it even more (sort of).

Being a one-man band and creating simple videos is perfect for situations like vlogging. However, if you're ready to move up from fixed-focus webcam vids that are often about as exciting as dipping french fries in ketchup, you will need to consider stepping things up a notch.

Unless you live in some kind of fairytale land, videos don't just magically appear as if pulled from some magician's hat. Creating videos requires proper planning, execution and a wee bit of luck. Of course, 'luck' is often a variable that is hard to quantify and often eludes even the purest of heart. But let me let you in on a little secret, if you're prepared and know what to expect, luck's portion of the equation for success can be reduced significantly.

Video planning in advance is known as *pre-production*. The more you know about your project, the better your chance of troubleshooting problems before they occur.

1.

First and foremost, you need to know what kind of video you are creating. If it's the kind of video that requires a script, you need to have that completed before you record a single frame. Don't buy into the stories of creative juices flowing on set that magically allow you to make it up as you go along. Sure, it happens, but it is rare and not the best idea.

In fact, you should endeavor to have your script complete before you begin your pre-production.

A script is the blueprint for your video. It informs you of the resources and locations you will need and the types of people and characters who will appear on camera.

Don't get hung up on proper formatting and spending a ton of money on screenplay writing software. A good script has all the dialogue, settings and characters in it. Beyond that, how detailed you get is up to you.

2.

If your project isn't to be so "scripted," you should at the very least create an outline. Knowing what kind of locations you need and the type of things that need to be said on camera should all be down on paper before you begin shooting.

Professionals plan. So should you. What pros have is experience. If experience teaches someone they need to plan in advance, then that should be considered a very valuable lesson to take to heart. By failing to prepare, you are preparing to fail.... Know who said that? Benjamin Franklin. That guy tied a key to a kite in a rainstorm and you'd better believe he didn't just do it on a whim.

Don't let the universe surprise you... the universe is often unkind. There's another word for it: gambling. No one wins every time they gamble!

3.
Make a list of all the resources you will need. This may include: actor/hosts, crew, a location, lights, camera, microphones, props or memory cards for your camera.

Never assume that you can just grab and go on the day you plan to film. Our parents told us all more than once what happens when you assume.

If you don't know or are unsure what kind of equipment you need you will need to consult with someone who does.

4.
Hire a cameraman. If you're lucky, the cameraman you hire will have all of his own equipment (and possibly helpers). If you are paying the cameraman a fee, make sure it's all-inclusive. No need being surprised when they hand you a bill full of add-ons.

Keep in mind that as with all freelancers, each cameraman (or camerawoman) you hire will have their own rates. Some charge by the hour, but most will give you a half-day and full-day rate to choose from. Always make sure to ask to see their previous work (known as a reel) to get a feel for what their style and skills really are.

Anyone can look good in a proposal.

5.
When renting equipment, try to do so from a reputable source. Check everything out before you take it home. Make sure you know exactly when it has to be returned.

Don't have a local resource to do this? No worries because there are many online rental shops that will ship the equipment directly to you. Two of our favorites are <u>Lens Pro to Go</u> and <u>Borrow Lenses</u>.

6.
Secure a location. If your cameraman needs to check out your location first, make sure they know what they're working with.

In some places, your shoot location may require you to have a permit. If you shoot where a permit is required and you don't have one, you could get shut down by the cops, and I doubt your cameraman or your equipment rental company will offer you any refunds.

7.
Make sure your location is mostly controllable, safe and external noise is not an issue. Be sure you visit the location at the same time of day you are planning to film so you know where the sun shines. You'd be amazed how different your perfect location looks in the morning compared to dusk.

Always know where electric lines can be plugged in and if the location's wiring can handle all the stuff you're planning to plug into it. Unless you're shooting "Backdraft 2", keep the fire department away from your set.

8.

Are you planning to shoot on a green or blue screen and then key in your background in editing? This type of shooting has specific lighting requirements that may require additional rentals or hiring of professionals.

Also, make sure your green/blue screen is big enough to handle the type of shots you're looking for. You need more space than you think you do. Never forget that.

9.

Will you need a teleprompter or cue cards? Not sure? Ask the talent that will be on screen how they usually work with lines.

Big white poster board from an office supply store will work great. There are also many apps that can be installed on your tablet to do this as well.

10.

Schedule a date for your shoot and then cast your project for that date. Unless you're working with a big star, booking your crew and location(s) should be your first scheduling consideration.

11.

A smart video producer will make sure that anyone they put in front of a camera has signed a release that grants permission and rights to the material that is shot. You can find talent-release forms online. Just make sure whichever one you use covers all the possible ways you intend to use your video for the immediate and long-term future.

Don't get stuck not being able to re-use your video on television when your budgets get bigger because your release was for online use only. Trust us, it happens more than you might think. Always double check.

12.

Make schedules for everything. If there are any costs involved, make a (reasonable) budget. Try to determine your costs for everything upfront so you can stay within your budget.

13.

Most importantly, don't forget to provide lunch for everyone. It doesn't have to be fancy, let your conscience be your guide. Happy stomachs = happy shoot.

14.

Mistakes sometimes make for good learning tools, but nothing beats doing it right the first time.

15.

If you have the luxury of time and unlimited resources, experiment all you want on your own dime. If all you're doing is putting a camera up on a tripod and rolling indefinitely until something magical happens, then go knock yourself out.

If you want to create something more structured, you will need to embrace pre-production as a necessary step toward succeeding.

16.
Now take a deep breath. You've just taken the first big leap toward producing your first real video.

Pre-production may not be the most glamorous or fun part of the process, but it should be very rewarding to realize how much more interesting things are going to get from here. Seats back up and tray tables locked in the upright position.

Next up: Lights, camera... action! Let's shoot!

≈ PRO TIP ≈
STEVE GARFIELD

Planning before shooting video doesn't have to be complicated. You can even plan your shot in the time it takes to take your iPhone out of your pocket. What you need to think about is the end result, what are people going to see. I know it sounds pretty simple, but many times I'll see people holding up their cameras with their hand and moving it up and down, side to side, holding it too low... These are all things that you can think about before pressing the record button.

My main tips would be:

Number one:
Know your camera. You need to be able to press record and be confident that you are going to get a good quality video you will be able to save and share.

Number two:
If it's an interview make the interviewee comfortable so he or she forgets there's even a camera there. Have a conversation with the interviewee and sit just behind, a little offset from the camera.

Number three:
Shoot and share. One of the main problems with interviews, for example, are they get done and then they never see the light of day because you plan to

edit it and get it up at some point and you want to make it perfect. Don't do that. Try shooting quick short interviews and posting them immediately to social media like YouTube or Facebook. It doesn't have to be perfect. It just has to get shared.

Steve Garfield, Videoblogging pioneer, Investor and Advisor. SteveGarfield.com

≈ PART 2 ≈
SHOOT YOUR VIDEO LIKE A PRO

Finally, the moment where the magic really begins.

Unless you're operating a security camera, your shoot isn't going to happen at random. In order to allow your cast and crew to shine and give you their very best, your shoot needs to be set up as the proper environment for success.

Even if it is just you and your camera, you'll be more successful if you keep these things in mind.

17.
The day of your shoot, arrive early. That is job number one.

It doesn't matter how much or how little you are involved with the filming process, if it's your video project you will be best served by arriving at your location before everyone else. That way if anyone else, like cast or crew, or perhaps someone delivering something important shows up, they'll be able to get answers and won't be left sitting around on your dime.

Plus, by being there first, anything wrong or different than you were hoping for can be addressed immediately, and hopefully before more people arrive.

18.
Setting up for your video may be as simple as getting your gear plugged in, your memory card formatted and your tripod in place. Then again, it could be a lot more complicated.

Hopefully, you and your crew established an accurate setup window when negotiating. Every task has a minimum amount of time it will take to be camera-ready. Always schedule accordingly and make sure every crew and cast member knows his or her call time. Few things are more aggravating on set than having everything ready to go and then having to wait for someone.

19.
If properly scouted, your location shouldn't provide you with any surprises (such as where the electricity can be found). Most likely you are going to need lights of some kind. Thanks to those lights, makeup is almost always a consideration.

This isn't just for women on camera. Men you've got to think about it as well. Sure, you can skip the makeup and shoot a great video, but any professional video you've watched involved makeup.

Even to look natural, like they're not wearing makeup, people on camera generally need to actually wear makeup. Yes, it's an injustice. If you don't like it go on the Internet and complain.

20.

You will need access to bathrooms. Trees and back alleys don't count! Don't let this consideration get lost in your planning.

Also don't forget that you should always provide clean drinking water and food as well. Check ahead of time with everyone involved to find out if any of them have dietary restrictions. Nothing worse than showing up on set with all-you-can-eat bacon only to find out your crew is vegan.

Set up a table, cooler or area as early as possible. Make sure it doesn't run out. Your cast and crew work hard.

Tiny candy bars are good energy boosters that don't take too long to consume. Just don't forget to clean up your trash.

21.

Double check. Has your talent signed their on-camera releases? Do you have legal rights to use everything you are shooting today? Do you need a teleprompter or cue cards? These are all things to know beforehand in order to spare yourself costly delays.

22.

Get your microphones ready. Check your audio levels. Make sure you have audio levels.

If you are using a microphone that requires batteries, have plenty of backups on hand. If you are recording audio to an external audio recorder instead of direct to camera, make sure that device has plenty of memory/recording time and battery power, too.

Audio is almost more important than video because no matter how pretty it may look, if people can't hear what is being said it won't matter.

23.
Check your lighting one last time to make sure it's right. Bad lighting could cost you time during editing. Really bad lighting could ruin your takes.

24.
Quiet on set.

25.
Once everything is in place and ready to go, cross your fingers and hit the record button.

Double check that you are recording. Nothing worse than getting a great take and realizing that you didn't capture it.

26.
Slate everything you shoot at the beginning of each take. Even if your audio is recorded in the camera and already synced to video, marking your takes makes it much easier to find what you need and saves time during editing.

Don't have your own slate? A small whiteboard will allow you to write the details of the take down and then you can clap your hands. It isn't high-tech but it works on a budget.

27.

Let the camera roll for a couple of seconds to make sure everything is settled and quiet... then cue your talent to begin... "action!"

28.

Once the take is complete, don't turn off the recording right away. Let the camera run for a couple of seconds to ensure you're not cutting off the end of a good performance.

Few things are worse than getting into the editing suite and finding out that you cut off that last line of the perfect take.

29.

Don't be afraid to ask for another take, if only just for coverage.

In fact, you never want just one take. Always get a second one. No exceptions.

30.

Keep a list of all the takes you felt were really good. Don't lose this.

31.

Let your cast and crew do their thing. If you don't like a take, reset and do it again. If you're not getting the magic you're looking for, stop and talk with your cast/crew. Don't be afraid to give specific direction if you know what you want.

Remember: they can't read your mind.

32.
If something goes wrong, don't lose your cool.
Calmly try to fix it or find a way around it. Something always goes wrong and it'll hopefully make for good laughs later.

Always keep a roll of duct tape handy. Duct tape can fix almost anything on a film set. (and in life)

33.
Whatever you do, don't yell. Don't lose your temper.

Some creatives may have more delicate sensibilities than you. You want the best performance out of your cast and crew, so tread lightly on their nerves. Maintain your cool throughout the shoot.

If you have any issues you need to work out on set, do it in a way that won't bring your shoot to a grinding halt. Bigger issues with people can, and should, be worked out after the shoot is over.

34.
That being said, when you need something done, be firm... just don't be a jerk about it.

35.
Record room tone. Every location has its own unique, subtle, low-volume sound signature -- what you hear when everything is silent.

With your cast and crew in place. Ask everyone to stand completely silent for two minutes (not checking email or Facebook, silent) and record the quiet sound of the room. This is important for audio continuity in case you need your overdubs and edits to match the room ambience in post-production.

Whether you do it first or last, record room tone. One bit of advice, because it's easy to forget to do it once you've finished shooting, it may be a good idea to record room tone FIRST, before your first take.

If you are filming in multiple locations, even if it is two different rooms in the same building, you need to capture room tone for all of them.

36.
If you have to change locations/setups, make sure you've allowed for that in your schedule. Because of the gremlins that often appear when there are cameras present, don't be surprised if unforeseen delays occur.

37.
Breaks in between setups and takes are good times to check your camera. Every so often make sure you have enough recording time available on your camera. Check your battery levels and the amount of tape/memory you have left. Hopefully, you brought backups and spares.

Don't let your batteries run until they're dead. When you switch out batteries, plug in the ones you've just removed so they can begin recharging.

38.
This is important: DO NOT run your memory cards completely full. You could potentially corrupt the

card and render it unreadable, ruining all of your
other takes that are on it.

39.
When you put in a new tape/memory card, switch the
removed media's "copy protect" to *on*. It's usually a
small slider on one side that will make sure nobody
else can record on that media while it's protected.

You wouldn't be the first person to record over
something you didn't want to lose, but we'd rather
you didn't find out the hard way what that's like.

40.
Schedule short breaks every couple of hours, if
possible. 15 minutes to clear your mind can help keep
things on the rails. Plus, your cast and crew will
remain fresh by doing this.

41.
If and when you take an extended break for lunch or
a new setup, check if you have enough time to make a
copy of your footage onto a hard drive. You will
eventually have to do this for editing and long breaks
offer a good chance to get ahead of the curve so
you're not doing it all later, after the shoot, when you
may be fatigued.

A best practice would be to do this any time you
remove media from the camera if possible. You can
start the backup process and go back to shooting if
needed.

No matter when you do it, you need to make backups/copies of your footage. You expended resources and time to acquire it; don't let it get lost.

42.

Before you declare the shoot to be wrapped up, double and triple check to make sure you have shot everything you were supposed to shoot. Look over the list you've been keeping and compare it to your script or outline.

43.

When your shoot is done, thank everyone for his or her hard work. Again, you can deal with individual concerns with people's performance/ attitude later. Now's not the time for anything but praise.

44.

Make sure everything is packed up properly. Double and triple check that you have all of your footage with you.

45.

Pay your crew. If your cast requires payment, take care of that, too. If, for tax purposes, you need folks to fill out W-9 or any other tax forms, make sure they do that before they leave.

Whenever possible have them fill out all needed paperwork before the shoot happens. No one wants to sit around after a long day of filming filling out forms if they don't have to.

46.
Double-check any rental equipment to make sure you have everything that came with it that you need to return. Also make sure to return it on time so you don't have to pay extra.

Walk the perimeter of the room you are filming in for one last check of power outlets to be sure you didn't leave something plugged in.

Don't be afraid to make a checklist of all the above considerations. Anybody who laughs at you for being diligent has probably never been in your shoes.

Hopefully, at this point you can reflect upon your shoot and how well it went (or at least well enough to get everything you needed).

Now comes the next step, assembling your first edit!

≈ *PRO TIP* ≈
KEN FLEISCHER

I've found that most people new to video production usually try to do too much. It's always going to take longer than you expect.

Start simple, a basic talking head, a simple interview, and two shot, slowly expand your options as you get comfortable.

Take the time to setup your shots, the same way you'd take the time to setup a photo.

Good framing, cleaning lighting, sharp focus, and clear audio, each one can make a big difference in the quality of your videos.

Make videos for your audience, not your industry. Nobody outside of a conference room talks in marketing speak or industry terms.

Plain language and a genuine approach, talk in terms you are certain your audience uses every day.

Ken Fleischer, dMworks - Writer, Director, Producer of Video, Film, Advertising and Motion Graphics.

≈ *PRO TIP* ≈
MITCH JOEL

In all of this video stuff, don't forget about the quality of the audio. Try to ensure that the audio is recorded so that whoever hears it... can feel it. Make sure the voices, the music, the sounds feel like they are inside my brain. If there is motion and external sounds, make it feel like I am physically there with you. Don't rely solely on the microphones that are built into these cameras and smartphones. More often than not, they're bad. Invest in the audio to ensure all of the viewers' senses stay attracted.

Mitch Joel, President, Twist Image – Author, *Six Pixels of Separation* and *CTRL ALT Delete*

≈ *PART 3* ≈

EDIT YOUR VIDEOS WITH CONFIDENCE

Editing is the phase of video production that breathes life into your project. There are few moments in the process as exciting as watching the playback of the first cut of your video.

Just know that editing, like every other step of video creation, is a process. Rushing through it with sloppy results can ruin the best footage. Conversely, a great editing job can make footage that isn't quite perfect seem brilliant when constructed with care and a discerning eye.

47.

By now you have transferred all of your shot footage onto a hard drive. Oh, you haven't yet? Lather, rinse, repeat. We'll wait.

Make sure whatever hard drive you use is of recent vintage and good working order. Refer to whoever is editing your video or your editing software to make sure the hard drive and editing system are compatible. If this sounds obvious, you'd be surprised how many times people make this mistake.

Hard drives are not expensive, so consider getting a second one to be able to make a safety back up of all your raw footage. Set it aside for emergencies.

48.

Editing is a resource-consuming beast. Not only does every physical act of editing require time, but so does every action that requires a computer to render in order to proceed. Any duration that the computer is transferring, rendering, loading or doing whatever else computers tend to do in their own sweet time, it's that much longer until your project is finished. If you're paying for editing time you'll rue each of those lost minutes and seconds.

Everything we're telling you here today is to help you save as much time in the edit bay as possible.

The next thing you need to know from your editor/ editing software is the video format that will be most compatible. It may differ from the format of the raw video transferred from the camera. If you have to convert formats, you should first make backups, just in case. Next, try to do those conversions before you go into editing in order to prevent having to do those tasks on the editor's time. Lastly, like all matters technical, if you don't know how to do this, consult with someone experienced.

49.

Okay, you have the right format for the right software for the right system. Mark that hard drive and keep it safe.

Optimally, you want to have copies of your takes that you can preview before you go into editing. I know you have your notes from the shoot that detail the best takes, but these are just breadcrumbs to lead us to all the good stuff.

50.
Try to preview all of your noted "good" takes. Double-check your initial instincts. Compile your shot list. Make note of what part in each take contains footage you want to use, or at least plug in, during editing.

While you're at it, watch all the other takes, too if you have the time. You never can tell what you may have missed in the heat of the moment. Hidden gems sometimes hide where you least expected to find them.

51.
You always want to go into editing at least having some semblance of an idea what you're looking for. Try to take note of any trouble spots in the lighting or audio that will need to be fixed later.

52.
Shot list complete? Got all your notes? Good, now it's time to begin cutting and splicing!

53.
Assemble your best shots. Get in late and get out early. Tell a story.

54.
Most computer-based editing is "non-destructive" which means that you can use can use portions of a take without altering the original file.

In the olden days of film, this type of thing required a razor blade and splicing tape. Those were edits that were more difficult to undo.

With non-destructive editing you can pick and chose what you need from each take without hacking your original takes to shreds. This also means that if you screw things up, you can always fix it and all you cost yourself was time.

55.
If you're not sure where to begin, just go shot by shot from your script or outline and start there. As you begin putting them together, your story should become more obvious.

56.
Most computers these days come with some kind of basic editing software built in. Truth is, the more professional software solutions are not that different from their consumer-level counterparts, they just have more features and more things to tweak under the hood. They mostly use the same type of drag-and-drop architecture.

Whatever editing software you use, be sure that whoever is doing the editing knows what they are doing. If this task falls on your shoulders be sure that you've learned the basics of how to use it so your project isn't delayed while you are learning.

57.
Don't go crazy with transitions between shots. Use them only when you need them. Sometimes definitive transitions between scenes help improve pacing.

Remember, a starburst wipe rarely does anything more than annoy your viewer.

58.
Record any overdubs that are necessary. The reason you recorded all that room tone is to make sure the ambiences match.

59.
Add in sound effects and music, if needed. Mix your audio tracks accordingly. You never want to bury dialogue tracks so they can't be understood.

Make sure you secure all the needed licensing for any music you use. We respect music and so should you.

60.
Here's the first real pro-audio trick for your bag of tricks. Using audio compression on your master audio tracks can help even up your audio levels so they're not all over the place.

Give it a try. If it doesn't work, you don't have to compress your audio, it's just a recommendation. Try not to use too much compression, or it will sound unnatural.

61.
Once you have a complete cut of the body of your video that includes final audio, you can add any bumpers, opening or closing title cards or title sequences you have.

As you continue to create episodes, you can make a template that allows you to easily drop in your opening and closing bumpers with one click.

Don't worry if you have no idea how to create these. Most editing programs can create basic (and sometimes advanced) ones for you. If you can't create one you want, again you'll need to hire someone who specializes in motion graphics to create them for you.

62.
If you have the time, live with your edit for a day. Preview it for a few people whose opinion you respect.

Editing is often a wearying task and sometimes a good night's sleep will help you look at everything with fresh eyes.

63.
If you're working with an experienced editor, listen to their advice. **A good editor is both a craftsman and an artist.** You are paying for their expertise, so trust them.

Like everything else, the more you do it, the better you'll get... but you have to start somewhere and once you've edited your first video, you'll be looking forward to your next one.

Up Next... Your edit looks great. Now let's make a master copy and put copies on the Internet for all to see.

≈ *PRO TIP* ≈
ANN HANDLEY

1. Create a title that says how you feel, not just what it is.

Your video's title is like a headline on a story. Be truthful about what your video is about (don't try to trick people into watching it), but try to give people a deeper sense of why this video is worth watching. And be specific. Speak to your viewer by using "you" instead of "we" or "I."

*So if your video is a tutorial on vegan cupcakes, don't just play it straight with something like **A Step by Step Approach to Making Vegan Cupcakes**.*

*Instead, tell us how you feel, give us a sense of why this video is different, and why it matters. Maybe: **The Best Vegan Cupcakes You'll Ever Taste**. Or, **How to Make Vegan Cupcakes That Don't Taste Like They're Vegan**.*

A great title will help you market your video by being really clear on what it's about, and why it matters to viewers.

2. Don't create just a one-off video. *Plan a series people can subscribe to; have a bigger plan. You might get lucky and attract a bunch of attention with single video (Dollar Shave Club sure did!). But* *don't plan on it. You're much better off planning a long-term series than a one-hit wonder.*

Ann Handley, Chief Content Officer - MarketingProfs.com
& AnnHandley.com

≈ *PART 4*≈

GETTING YOUR VIDEOS ONLINE THE RIGHT WAY

Your video has been fully edited (and quite possibly re-edited). Don't worry, first edits are often like that first batch of pancakes that come out a bit lumpy around the edges.   Sometimes it takes a little finessing to get *just* right.

But, at some point you'll have a finished product you are happy with, and now it is time to get it up on the web for everyone else to be able to view and share it.

64.
Now that your video is done (or if you've hit the point where the editor is kicking you out), you need one big thing before you leave the edit bay: a master copy.

This will be a fully rendered digital copy of your video with the least amount of compression that is practical. QuickTime movies using the Apple ProRes 422 (HQ) OR Animation codes are good for making masters that are widely compatible.

You may also choose to render a master copy to some type of digital tape. Digital tape is a very cost-effective backup method if it is available to you.

65.

While it may seem like a great idea to take home your master copy as a DVD or BluRay disc, remember that you will have to use your master to make derivative copies.

Ripping video off of DVD's is fairly simple, but time consuming, so you're better off with a digital copy of a file as your main master and a DVD as something you can use to preview your video later.

66.

On Final Cut Pro and other video editing programs, the command you're looking for is EXPORT or SHARE.

67.

If you shot in HD, render your master at the same resolution as it was shot and edited. Upscaling 720 to 1080 may lead to less than desirable results so don't do it.

68.

For your master copy, the most preferable output is the output with the least amount of compression. Uncompressed files tend to be a lot bigger than you may think. Your final uncompressed video may take up several gigabytes when rendered. If this is the case and your final render is huge, there's a good chance your computer may not be able to play it back smoothly.

That's okay, because now that our master copy has been rendered for safe keeping we're going to make copies we can actually watch and upload.

69.

Back up your master copy to an external hard drive. **Make a backup copy of your master.** This new copy will be the one we clone to make sure we don't corrupt the master, which is now archived safely where it can be found if needed.

70.

If you are making a copy for YouTube, Vimeo or other streaming sites, there are some render settings to help your video look as good as possible online.

MP4 or MPEG-4
This is one of the most universally-used formats. We would suggest making all of your distribution copies MP4.

Audio Codec: AAC-LC
This will help keep your quality high and your audio files small. Keep it stereo (or Stereo 5+1) if you've mastered your audio in surround. Use the 48khz sample rate setting. Set your audio bitrate to 384.

Video Codec: H264

BitRate: 5,000kbps for 720. 8,000 for 1080.

Also, you will want to **Deinterlace** your final rendered video for online uploading. Interlacing is only something you need for copies that are either broadcast or shown on TV.

Also use **Progressive Scan** settings. These can be achieved by choosing resolution settings that end in the letter 'p', such as "1080p" or "720p." Progressive scanning helps create a more detailed image that is less susceptible to flicker.

High quality HD upload copies will help ensure your video looks best. Technology has a way of updating rapidly. All those videos shot and uploaded in standard definition just a few years ago look quite boxy and Stone Age now.

71.
Now you have your online-ready copy ready for upload to the Internet. Before other people can watch your masterpiece online, your video will need to be "hosted" somewhere. That means it has to be uploaded in a way that it can easily be played back, and/or downloaded.

72.
We recommend that you put your video on YouTube and Vimeo at a minimum. Both sites make placing your video online very simple.

Their interface allows for drag-and-drop uploading. Fill in the information boxes in the upload window and wait for your video to be swallowed up onto their server and rendered for playback.

73.
The overall best place, however, to have your audience find you is your own branded online destination, your own website. If you have compatible web hosting for your site, you can also upload a copy to your own server.

If that isn't an option, all video hosting sites make it easy for you to embed a copy of the video from their site onto yours.

74.
As you may have noticed, videos (especially in HD) can be quite large, which means they eat up a lot of bandwidth when played back. If you have a tiny hosting plan for your website and get a lot of downloads, you may find that your hosting company has turned off your account, or is charging you extra for all the additional bandwidth. Check your hosting account for details.

Yet another reason to use a site like Vimeo or YouTube for hosting your video is because they're bandwidth is provided to you for free.

75.
If you are uploading your video to a video-sharing website, first make sure your video doesn't violate their Terms of Service (TOS). If your video is made up of all original work you should be okay as long as the subject matter is allowed on their site.

76.
Once your video has been uploaded and is ready for playback, watch the whole thing again from start to finish. That way if you find a glitch in the upload, you can fix it by trying to upload again before you start telling people your video is ready to be seen.

If you continue to have issues with the playback of an uploaded video, there may be an issue with your upload file, or it may be corrupted. Go back to your master and render another upload copy and try again.

77.

One thing to note: while you may be tempted to use music from other artists in your video, you need to first have permission from that artist (and most likely the permission of the music publishing company that administrates the song's rights).

The use of other people's work without permission can not only get your video taken down, but it could get you sued. If you have any questions about rights and usage, the safest bet is to consult with someone familiar with copyright law. YouTube is notorious for quickly taking down videos with unlicensed content.

Now that your video is online you have to get people to watch it. But they can't watch it if they don't know about it. Next up, let's get the word out!

≈ PRO TIP≈
CASEY NEISTAT

Story. All that matters is story. Viewers will forgive bad sound, bad cinematography, and weak editing so long as you tell a great story and tell it well. That, and use a tripod, nobody likes shaky camera.

Casey Neistat, Film director, producer and creator of popular YouTube videos since 2010.
CaseyNeistat.com

≈ PART 5 ≈
HOW TO MARKET YOUR ONLINE VIDEO

You've done it. Congratulations! The video you planned out and worked hard to produce is shot, edited and you've uploaded it online. These are big steps. Honestly, you've gotten much further than a lot of people who would like to be in your shoes but never get this far because of poor planning, lack of resources or simply because they're working their way up to hitting this milestone.

So take a moment to pat yourself on the back. **Now take a deep breath because, as some may say, this is where the real work begins.**

It's one thing to have a video; it's another thing entirely to have a video that is being *seen* by others.

78.
First off, let's dispel the myth that the mere act of dumping your video on YouTube ensures it will be discovered by others.

According to YouTube's own press page, *72 hours of video content is uploaded to the site every minute!* That is unbelievably horrifying. Let me make it even more disconcerting. That means your 4 minute long video makes up less than one-tenth of one percent of what is being uploaded every 60 seconds.

Okay, we are not here to bum you out, but knowing the facts of what you're up against will help you make better informed choices and hopefully, save you valuable time and resources in the long run.

79.
Giant video sharing sites like YouTube are not meant to be used as discovery mechanisms. You may be hanging your hopes that your video thumbnail will appear in the sidebar for searches related to your content, and if your video is about something popular it probably will... along with many other videos on the same topic.

80.
The "build it and they will come" theory only really works if you're the first (or among the first).

There's a great story about what happened after Lana Turner was discovered by a movie agent while sipping a Coke at the counter of Schwab's drug store on Hollywood Boulevard. The next day, and every day after for quite a long time, the store was mobbed by Lana Turner lookalikes hoping the same fortune would strike them. It didn't quite work out the same for those who were trying to shoehorn into a trend.

81.
Piggybacking on someone else's viral hit will only get you so far. What it does do, however, is paint your brand as a follower, not a leader. Think about it.

Once you get going and have a few videos under your belt you can always create separate videos that are specific reactions to other successful videos and then link to them. This isn't a terrible way to get noticed, but please note that this is NOT a viable, top-line strategy for success, just an extra honeypot you can set out to catch more flies.

82.

And while we're at it, let's talk about trying to create "viral" videos. Viral videos happen like a lightning strike. You cannot expect to manufacture a viral video.

Those videos that go from obscurity to millions of views overnight are often blessed with the strange alchemy of incident and achievement with a dash of timing. Know that you can, however, increase your chance of making your video go viral if you already have a large audience conditioned to share your content with their friends.

83.

And it will be your friends that will light the fuse on this rocket. Getting the word out about your amazing new video begins with your social circle. Begin with those closest to you, people you know personally and not just online. Send a nice email announcing how proud you are to be unveiling a new project. Mention how much everyone's support during the whole process has been. Even if this is the first time some of these folks are hearing about your video, as long as they're your "inner circle" they'll appreciate being thanked anyway, because, let's face it, there's probably a good chance that they've already done something to support you in the past, right?

Tell your amazing friends where to find your video...
Now, I'm going to put a pin in this for a brief moment
to talk to you about how critically important this next
part is for your strategy.

84.
YouTube, Vimeo and other video sharing sites are
fine places to host your video. Hey, who doesn't like
free bandwidth, right? HOWEVER, branding and
marketing experts will tell you that the smartest
destination to drive your audience to is your own
branded website.

Giant walled electronic gardens like YouTube are not
designed to keep your audience focused on your
content, as much as they are designed to just keep the
viewer on the site watching as much video as is
possible, regardless of whether it's yours or not.
There is no guarantee they won't be distracted by
something else and either forget what your video was
all about, or not even watch it at all.

85.
When you have your own branded website, you're
telling the audience more about you, your brand,
maybe your business. If you are creating video in
order to further some agenda, like getting yourself or
your business noticed, having that potential future
fan consume your content from your site will result in
much stronger engagement with that audience
member.

When viewers are surrounded by your brand, it
makes a deeper impression and improves retention

(like having a .tv domain to instantly inform the audience that there's video to check out here).

Let us ask you a different question. Would you rather meet with Steven Spielberg in your quiet office, or in the middle of Grand Central Station?

86.

So now you're telling those amazing friends to come to your site to check out your video. But that's not enough; you have to tell them that they need to tell their other friends about it, too.

Of course, *tell* is what you need to do, *suggest politely* is what your friends need to feel you're doing. Make an honest plea for social sharing, cash in your karma chips and let it roll. Never assume that friends will automatically share what you've created.

87.

Okay, now comes the 2nd level of notifications. Think of everybody you know who, in your opinion, is some kind of bigwig. Think of anyone your friends happen to know.

Network president. Talent manager. Local Reporter. Someone who knows how to shake the ground a little bit.

88.

Before you pull the trigger on that just know: your video better be really great and you'll probably only get one shot at impressing this contact.

Be professional. Be cool. Don't mess it up.

89.
Does your video have to do with some major current event? Do you have exclusive footage or content?

If it's newsworthy, contact your local TV news. You might get lucky. Author David Meerman Scott calls this "newsjacking."

90.
Now, if your video has to do with your business, think of any professional contacts you can send a link to. Does your industry have a trade group? Are there blogs or podcasts that cover your industry? Email your website links to these folks.

91.
Think of this next round of notifications as "mop up duty." Let's try to hit any last few promotional opportunities that won't cost us anything more than an email. Find any alumni groups you belong to that may have their own website, newsletter or Facebook Page.

92.
Social media is an amazing promotional tool -- a global marketplace of people you can reach for free. However, unlike mainstream media, you can repeat a single message only a small handful of times before people tune you out.

The key is to create a promotional strategy with the most potential for success. Spreading out promotional opportunities allows you to lengthen the conversation without sounding like a broken record. When you commence with your social media marketing, make a rollout plan of how you are going to talk about your video.

First, inform your core audience by posting the link (and a short description or call to action, if possible). Twitter is such a fast-moving beast that you should plan on posting it at least 3 times the first day -- once in the morning, afternoon and then at night -- in order to make sure you maximize your global reach across as many time-zones as possible.

93.
Facebook is different. Post your link to your page early. Make sure you are social that day. Like as much of your friends' stuff as you can stomach. Comment on stuff that isn't yours.

We know it sounds a bit like 'hiking up your skirt' to get a ride, but that's because it is. Welcome to social media.

94.
Speaking of Facebook Pages. Do a search for your video's subject matter on Facebook and find any related pages. Like them and post a link to your video and introduce yourself.

However, in the spirit of trying to lengthen the conversation as much as possible. Don't do this the first day. Start the second day of your launch and post to only 1 or 2 related pages a day. This helps keep your limited promotional cycle alive.

95.
Oh, and go post your link to Google+. You may be of the belief that Google+ isn't of any value to you, but what if, in the grand scheme of things, you ended up being wrong on that one. It'll take you a few moments. Just post it there and go. Can't hurt.

96.
For best results, do not try to announce your video to the world on a weekend or on a Monday.

There is no science here, but human nature says that most people have better things to do on their weekends than watch your video, and Mondays back in the office there are more distractions than any other day of the week.

97.
If you can somehow manage to keep your social media promotional efforts alive for a week without becoming a pariah, you deserve a medal. However, there is good news.

One week after you launch you have every right to re-launch and post again on your social networks. This time with the emphasis that your friends should definitely share this with their friends... because trust us, most people don't understand they should be doing it to begin with.

98.
Now, if your video has anything to do with the launch of a brand new show or channel, make a big deal out of it. Throw yourself a launch party. Make a big Facebook event out of it. This will also help keep your

stuff in the newsfeeds of potential fans and audience members.

99.
Last, but certainly not least, another thing you can piggyback promotions onto while getting people excited is a good contest. If you can think of one that relates to your video, give away something, a gift card, t-shirt, whatever. It'll help keep people thinking and talking about your brand.

100.
And if you have the time, cut yourself a 6-second teaser of your video and post it on Vine. Oh, your more of an Instagram person, you can upload up to a 15-second version there.

Hey, you never know?

And finally...

101.
Put that big imagination of yours to work and think of fun and creative ways to reach new people with your content. Marketing your video doesn't have to be a chore. **Remember, they can't watch your video if they don't know it's out there!**

≈ PRO TIP ≈
LYNETTE YOUNG

There is no easier or quicker way to build trust and rapport with your clients (and future clients) than by showing them your personality via online video. Google+ has given us "one-button" access to reaching the world. What are you waiting for? Let's see those pearly whites!

Lynette Young, Mar/Tech Professional and Google + Subject Matter Expert.
LynetteYoung.com

≈ *IT'S A WRAP!* ≈

Branding today is not about creating one good idea or one good slogan. It's about building a platform from which great ideas come from time and again. To make dollar one, you need faith more than you need trust. Faith that you are worth pulling out a wallet or checkbook that first time. Faith that you are worth talking about in an online status report that my friends will "Like."

If you, like us, have the desire to make video content for yourself, your brand and/or your business, you're not alone. We get it. You want lots of people to see, like and remember your ideas and messages, and more importantly, remember your name. You want to make an impression on people they will seldom soon forget. You see the current and future media landscape and know any decision to create videos is more important today than ever before.

One last thing... as long as your video subject matter dictates it, let your personality and individuality shine through.

Now go make some great videos!

C.C. & MYN

◇◇◇◇◇

ACKNOWLEDGEMENTS

First off, thank you to our all-star panel of Pros: Scott Monty, Ann Handley, Steve Garfield, Casey Neistat, Lynnette Young, Ken Fleischer and Mitch Joel for their wisdom and sage advice. Follow what these folks do and say online and you'll learn more in six months than any grad school could ever teach you.

Huge thanks to the Chapmans, the Nemcoffs and all of our extended families for the constant support of our creative endeavors, big and small.

Also to our friends and followers online for continuing to inspire us to create great content for you to enjoy!

And to all of you video creators out there, just know that thanks to the digital age, the sky is the limit!

Printed in Great Britain
by Amazon.co.uk, Ltd.,
Marston Gate.